Herbs, Spices & Fruits *of the* BIBLE

By Helga Curtis

HOUSE of
WHITE
BIRCHES

PUBLISHERS
SINCE 1947

Introduction

Designer Helga Curtis has selected herbs, spices and fruits found in the Bible as her theme to create these 15 unique appliqué blocks. The plants chosen range from cinnamon to garlic to figs. In addition to giving appliqué designs for each plant, Helga gives a Biblical reference for each one and shares interesting tidbits about the plant, such as how the spices were used both in Biblical times and also today.

Botanical prints were popular during the 18th century to decorate walls. In the same way, you will enjoy creating projects using these appliqué designs to decorate your home. Select several designs for a set of place mats for your kitchen table like is done with the onion, garlic, leek and shallot herbs as shown on the previous page. Or create a colorful wall quilt using the four fruit designs as shown on page 39. It's time to get started stitching.

General Instructions

Appliqué

Full-size patterns for the appliqué designs are included for each block in this book. Although basic hand-appliqué instructions are given with each project, you may use your favorite method of hand or machine appliqué to complete the designs.

Basic information and hints to help you successfully complete the blocks are given here. Read through these instructions before starting the blocks and refer to them as necessary. Any special instructions for a specific block are listed with the pattern.

Embroidery floss color, strand number and stitches are also indicated with each block, if required. Refer to instructions for Embroidered Details on page 5 to complete the stitches.

Preparing Fabrics

You will need a background fabric, leaf fabrics and fruit/herb/spice fabrics for each block. Refer to the Materials list for fabric colors suggested for the block.

If you prefer to use a machine-appliqué method, you will also need lightweight fusible web.

Each block requires a neutral-color background fabric. You may cut the background larger than listed in the Materials list or Cutting instructions, and after appliquéing the pieces trim to block size, plus seam allowances. A visually plain background allows the many small pieces of the flowers to stand out—tonal and mottled fabrics work well.

You will need a variety of small fabric pieces each block. Tonal prints, batiks and subtle multicolored prints will work well. Use care with solid fabrics—the larger pieces, such as leaves, will have no character without the shadings of the tonal prints or lines of the subtle prints. You may also find that solid fabrics will need additional embroidery for leaf veins or petal shadings to give them definition. Minimal yardage will also be suggested for borders.

Press the background square. Fold and crease to mark the block center. All patterns have a red centering mark to help with centering the design on the background.

Lightly trace the pattern on the background square using a water-erasable marker or chalk pencil. Trace only enough lines to help place your pieces as shown in Figure 1; do not trace every detail of the pattern.

Figure 1

Refer to the photos of each block to select colors for each piece. Color matches do not need to be precisely the same, but analyze the contrast and shadowing of each piece for a pleasing result.

When preparing templates and pieces for either hand or machine appliqué, be sure to include the section of a piece that will be overlapped by an adjacent piece. This section is outlined with dashed lines on the pattern as shown in Figure 2.

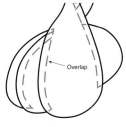

Figure 2

Embroidery details are also included on the patterns and need to be transferred to the templates and fabric pieces.

Hand Appliqué

For traditional hand appliqué, prepare a finished-size template from plastic. Trace the plastic templates on the right side of selected fabrics, allowing about ½" between pieces as shown in Figure 3. Cut out the pieces, adding ⅛"–¼" seam allowance to all edges, except those that will be overlapped by another piece. Turn under and hand-baste or glue-baste, with water-soluble fabric glue, the seam allowance of each piece or leave seam allowances to needle-turn as you appliqué the pieces.

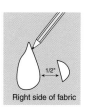

Right side of fabric

Figure 3

Freezer-Paper Techniques

To use freezer-paper templates on wrong side of fabric, photocopy or trace the design on a sheet of paper. Place the design side of the paper against a light box or bright window and trace the pieces on the paper side of freezer paper.

Cut out the pieces on the traced lines. Press the waxy side of the freezer-paper templates onto the wrong side of the selected fabric with a hot, dry iron, leaving space between pieces as shown in Figure 4. Cut out the pieces, adding ⅛"–¼" seam allowance to all edges, except those that will be overlapped by another piece. Press the seam allowance under using the edge of the freezer paper as a guide. Hand-baste in place through all layers to hold.

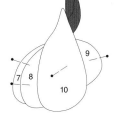

Wrong side of fabric

Iron

Figure 4   **Figure 5**

Beginning with the underneath pieces and working toward the foreground, pin or glue-baste the pieces in place on the background, overlapping pieces as indicated on the pattern as shown in Figure 5.

Blind-stitch the pieces in place, using thread to match the appliqué piece and turning under seam allowances, if necessary. Remove seam-allowance basting.

To remove freezer paper, cut a small slit in the background behind each appliquéd piece as shown in Figure 6. Remove the freezer-paper piece using small tweezers.

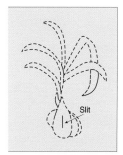

Slit

Figure 6

If darker pieces show through lighter top pieces, cut a slit through the background behind the darker piece and trim away the section of the darker piece that is overlapped by the lighter piece, leaving only a narrow seam allowance as shown in Figure 7. Trim the darker portion of the seam allowance, if necessary. Press the appliquéd design.

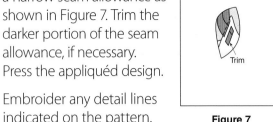

Figure 7

Embroider any detail lines indicated on the pattern. The floss color, number of strands and stitches are given with the pattern.

Trim the completed block to instructed size, if necessary.

To use freezer-paper templates on the right side of the fabric, trace the pattern pieces directly from the pattern onto the paper side of freezer paper. Cut out on traced lines and with a hot, dry iron, press pieces to the right side of selected fabrics.

Cut out pieces, adding ⅛"–¼" seam allowance to all edges, except those that will be overlapped by another piece.

Trace around all edges with a fabric marker of choice. Remove freezer paper and pin, thread-baste or glue-baste pieces to background, overlapping as indicated.

Needle-turn seam allowances, carefully including the traced line, as you blind-stitch in place.

Machine Appliqué

Fuse lightweight fusible interfacing to the wrong side of any light-color fabrics to prevent shadowing of darker fabrics.

Prepare a finished-size template from plastic for each piece in the design. Flip each template and trace the pieces to be cut from each fabric in a group on the paper side of lightweight fusible transfer web, leaving space between each fabric group as shown in Figure 8.

Figure 8

Instead of making templates, photocopy or trace the pattern onto another sheet of paper. Place the design side against a light box or bright window and trace the pieces to be cut directly onto the fusible transfer web, again grouping each fabric's pieces.

Roughly cut out each group of pieces, leaving approximately ¼" margin around each group. Fuse each group to the wrong side of the selected fabrics, following the manufacturer's instructions. Cut out each piece on the traced lines.

Beginning with the pieces farthest in the background or piece No. 1, remove the paper backing and arrange the pieces on the background in ascending order, overlapping pieces as indicated on the pattern. When satisfied with the arrangement, fuse pieces to the background fabric.

You may find it easier to fuse a pattern that has many pieces in small sections. Arrange one section in ascending order and fuse the pieces as shown in Figure 9. Move on to the next section and repeat. Continue fusing sections until the design is complete. Just remember to not only fuse the pieces within a section in ascending order, but to also fuse the pieces for the whole design in ascending order. Otherwise, you may find that you have fused a piece in one section that should have overlapped a piece in another section.

Figure 9

Cut a piece of fabric stabilizer large enough to fit behind the fused design. Fuse or pin it in place on the wrong side of the background square.

Use all-purpose thread, machine-embroidery thread or rayon thread to match each appliqué piece in the needle of your machine and all-purpose thread to match the background in the bobbin. Satin-stitch around the edges of each piece using a close medium-width stitch. Adjust your machine as necessary to prevent the bobbin thread from pulling to the top of your block.

Stitch detail lines as indicated on the pattern. Use satin or straight stitches or other decorative machine stitches to complete the detail lines.

Use a press cloth to press the appliquéd design. Trim the completed block to instructed size.

Embroidered Details

Embroidery is used to add details on many of the blocks. You may use machine or hand stitches to add these details. Special instructions for any embroidery are included for each block.

Embroider the details using the stitch suggestions given referring to the stitch illustrations below.

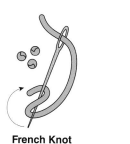
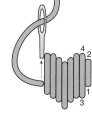

French Knot   **Satin Stitch**

Running Stitch

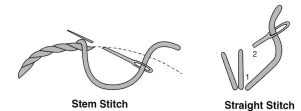

Stem Stitch   **Straight Stitch**

Finishing Your Quilt

When you have completed the quilt top as instructed with patterns, finish your quilt with these steps.

1. Sandwich the batting between the completed top and prepared backing piece; baste or pin to hold flat.

2. Quilt as desired by hand or machine. When quilting is complete, remove pins or basting.

3. Join the binding strips on short ends with a diagonal seam as shown in Figure 10; trim seam to ¼" and press open.

Figure 10

4. Cut the beginning end of the strip at a 45-degree angle as shown in Figure 11; press ¼" to the wrong side.

Figure 11

5. Fold the binding strip in half with wrong sides together along length; press.

6. Unfold the pressed angled end of the strip and anchor about 1" in place on the right side of the quilted project; refold and continue sewing both layers of the binding strip to the quilt, mitering corners and overlapping at the beginning and end as shown in Figure 12.

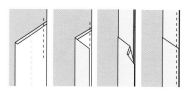

Figure 12

7. Turn the binding to the back side; hand-stitch in place to finish.

Mandrake

The mandrakes give off a fragrance, And at our gates are pleasant fruits, All manner, new and old, Which I have laid up for you, my beloved.

—Song of Solomon 7:13

Project Notes
The small motifs in the center of the mandrake design are fused rather than hand-appliquéd in place. Refer to Machine Appliqué fusible web techniques in the General Instructions for preparation of appliqué pieces 10–21. The pieces were not stitched after fusing, and since this is a project that probably won't require repeated washings, fusing without stitching is an acceptable method.

Project Specifications
Quilt Size: 17½" x 22½"

Materials
- Scraps light teal, lavender and purple solids
- Fat quarter green field print
- ⅛ yard yellow solid
- ⅓ yard brown mottled
- ⅜ yard yellow/green mottled
- Batting 22" x 27"
- Backing 22" x 27"
- All-purpose thread to match fabrics
- Quilting thread
- Yellow embroidery floss
- Water-erasable marker or chalk pencil
- Fabric glue stick
- Basic sewing tools and supplies

Cutting
1. Cut one 12½" x 17½" A rectangle green field print.

2. Cut two 1¼" by fabric width strips yellow solid; subcut strips into two 17½" B strips and two 14" C strips.

3. Cut two 2½" by fabric width strips yellow/green mottled; subcut strips into two 19" D strips and two 18" E strips.

4. Lightly trace each individual shape, excluding those prepared for fusible appliqué according to Project Notes, onto the right side of the fabrics as directed on pattern for color, adding extra at any areas that will be tucked under another piece.

5. Cut out shapes, adding ⅛"–¼" seam allowance all around for turning edges under.

6. Cut three 2¼" by fabric width strips brown mottled for binding.

Mandrake
Placement Diagram 17½" x 22½"

The mandrake plant grows in the fields of Israel and Syria and in places throughout the Mediterranean area, particularly Corsica. It is a perennial and related to the night shade, potato and tomato.

It is a stem-less herb with large leaves arranged in a rosette and purple flowers. The mandrake was a symbol of fertility. The yellow fruit has an unusual smell and sickeningly sweet taste.

Completing the Appliqué

1. Fold the A rectangle in half horizontally and vertically and crease to mark the center.

2. Turn edges of hand-appliqué shapes under along tracing lines; thread- or glue-baste to hold edges in place.

3. Referring to the Placement Diagram and the full-size pattern, arrange the pieces in place on center of the A background, overlapping as necessary; glue-baste, then hand-stitch in place using thread to match fabrics.

4. Add prepared fusible-appliqué pieces to the center following General Instructions.

Completing the Quilt

1. Using 2 strands of yellow embroidery floss and a stem stitch, add detail lines on leaves and French knots in the center of the flower.

2. Sew a B strip to opposite sides and C strips to the top and bottom of the stitched center; press seams toward B and C strips.

3. Sew D strips to opposite sides and E strips to the top and bottom of the stitched center; press seams toward D and E strips.

4. Layer, quilt and bind referring to Finishing Your Quilt on page 5. ●

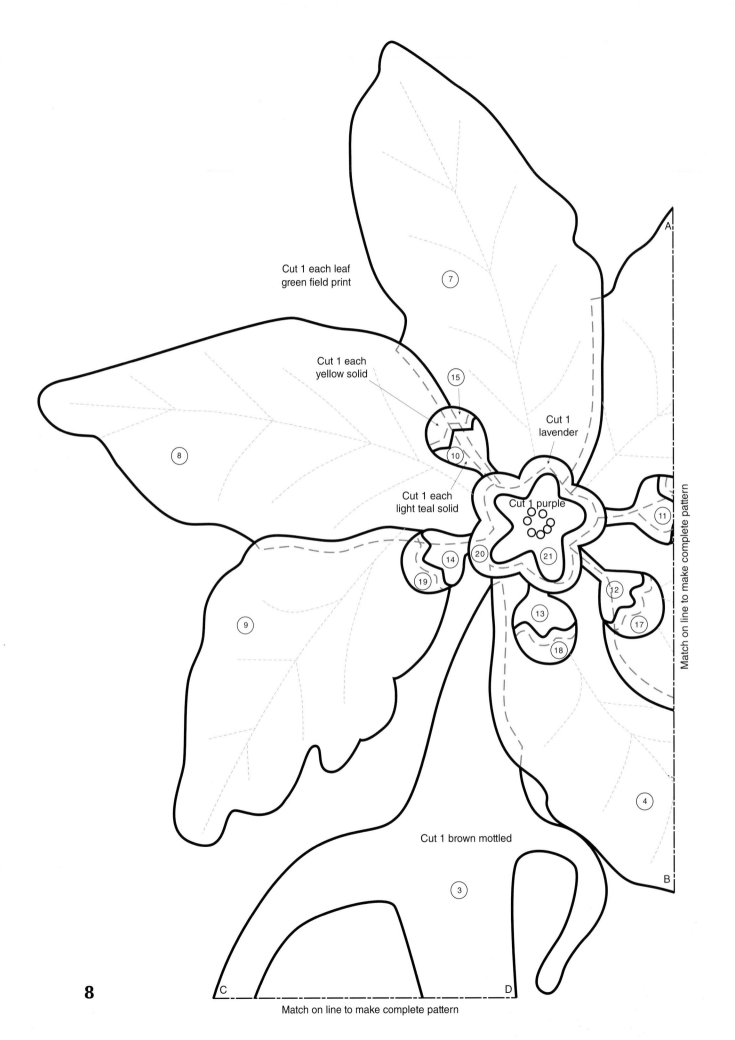

Cut 1 each leaf
green field print

Cut 1 each
yellow solid

Cut 1 each
light teal solid

Cut 1
lavender

Cut 1 purple

Cut 1 brown mottled

A

B

C

D

Match on line to make complete pattern

Match on line to make complete pattern

7

15

10

8

11

14

20

21

19

12

13

17

18

9

4

3

8

Match on line to make complete pattern

C   D

A

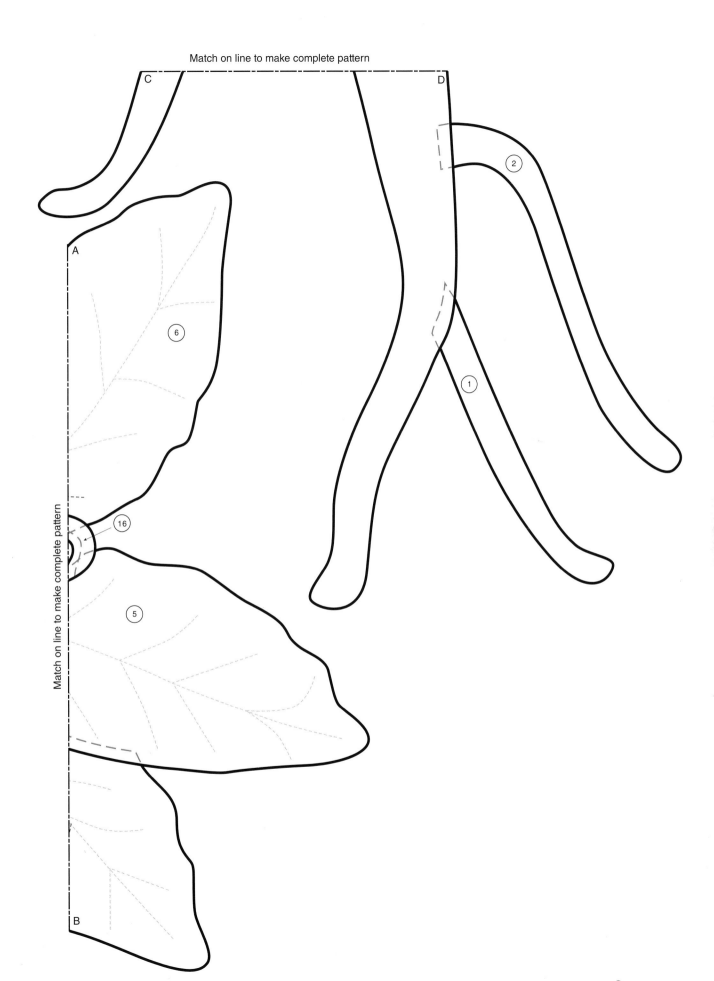

⑥

Match on line to make complete pattern

⑯

⑤

B

①

②

Chicory

Then they shall eat the flesh on that night; roasted in fire, with unleavened bread and with bitter herbs they shall eat it.

—Exodus 12:8

Chicory is known in the Bible as the bitter herb. It was used in a passover meal. It is a member of the endive family. Some varieties are cultivated for their roots. The roots are roasted, ground and added to coffee, chiefly in Louisiana.

Project Specifications
Quilt Size: 19" x 19"
Block Size: 13" x 13"

Materials
- Scraps dark green and blue tonals
- 4 (3½" x 3½") floral preprint C squares
- Fat quarter cream herb print
- Fat quarter cream batik
- ⅓ yard green leaf tonal
- Batting 23" x 23"
- Backing 23" x 23"
- All-purpose thread to match fabrics
- Quilting thread
- Medium blue embroidery floss
- Water-erasable marker or chalk pencil
- Fabric glue stick
- Basic sewing tools and supplies

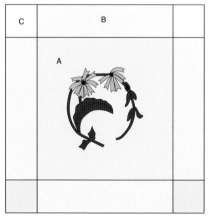

Chicory
Placement Diagram 19" x 19"

Chicory
13" x 13" Block
Make 1

Cutting
1. Cut one 13½" x 13½" A square cream batik.

2. Cut four 13½" x 3½" B strips cream herb print.

3. Lightly trace each individual appliqué shape for each of the three herb appliqué designs onto the right side of the fabrics as directed on pattern for color, adding extra at any areas that will be tucked under another piece.

4. Cut out shapes, adding ⅛"–¼" seam allowance all around for turning edges under.

Completing the Appliqué
1. Fold the A square horizontally and vertically and crease to mark the centers.

2. Turn edges of the appliqué shapes under along tracing lines; thread- or glue-baste to hold edges in place.

3. Referring to the block drawing and the full-size pattern, arrange the pieces in place on the center of the A background square, overlapping as necessary; glue-baste, then hand-stitch in place using thread to match fabrics.

4. Leave ends of blue flower petals unstitched, clip into the center and pull threads to make

a fringe on the end of each petal as shown in Figure 1. Add centers to the flowers using 2 strands blue embroidery floss and long straight stitches. Fill in the stitched teardrop shape with satin stitches and outline with stem stitches as shown in Figure 2.

Figure 1

Figure 2

Completing the Top
1. Sew a B strip to opposite sides of the stitched block; press seams toward B strips.

2. Sew a C square to each end of each remaining B strip; press seams toward B.

3. Sew a B-C strip to the remaining sides of the stitched block; press seams toward the B-C strips to complete the top.

Completing the Quilt
1. Layer, quilt and bind referring to Finishing Your Quilt on page 5. ●

Cut 1 each flower blue tonal scraps

Cut 1 each stem, teardrop (#11)
& leaf dark green tonal scraps

Chicory Appliqué Motif

12

Onion

We remember the fish which we ate freely in Egypt, the cucumbers, the melons, the leeks, the onions, and the garlic; but now our whole being is dried up; there is nothing at all except this manna before our eyes!

—Numbers 11:5-6

Project Specifications

Place Mat Size: 17½" x 11½"

Materials

- 1 (1¾" x 42") strip white mottled
- 6" x 6" square tan tonal
- 1 fat quarter medium green mottled
- ¼ yard white-with-blue dots
- ½ yard ⅛" blue-and-white gingham
- ½ yard ¼" blue-and-white gingham
- 1 (18" x 12") rectangle pre-washed flannel or lightweight batting
- All-purpose thread to match fabrics
- Quilting thread
- Green and gold embroidery floss
- Water-erasable marker or chalk pencil
- Fabric glue stick
- Template material of choice
- Basic sewing tools and supplies

Cutting

1. Cut one 12" x 18" rectangle each ⅛" (A) and ¼" (B) blue-and-white gingham.

2. Lightly trace the individual pattern pieces onto the right side of the fabrics as directed on pieces for color, adding extra at any areas that will be tucked under another piece. **Note:** *The top part of the onion used the wrong side of the tan tonal fabric as the right side to provide contrast. If using this method, trace those pieces onto the wrong side of the fabric.*

3. Cut out shapes, adding ⅛"–¼" seam allowance all around for turning edges under.

4. Cut two 2¼" by fabric width strips white-with-blue dots for binding.

Completing the Appliqué

1. Turn edges of appliqué pieces under along tracing lines; thread- or glue-baste to hold edges in place.

2. Referring to the Placement Diagram and full-size pattern for the motif, arrange the pieces in numerical order on the right side of A, at least ½" from the side and bottom edges of the left end; glue-baste to hold in place.

3. Hand-stitch edges of pieces in place using thread to match fabrics.

Making the Ruched Flowers

1. Fold under one end of the 1¾" x 42" strip ¼"; press. Fold the strip in half along length with wrong sides together and press lightly to crease. Open strip. Fold the top long edge of the strip to meet the creased line on the wrong side of the strip as shown in Figure 1; press. Repeat with the bottom edge of the strip as shown in Figure 2.

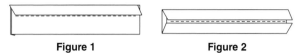

Figure 1   **Figure 2**

2. Mark a dot every inch on one edge of the folded strip. Mark ½" and then every inch on the opposite edge of the strip as shown in Figure 3.

Figure 3   **Figure 4**

3. Connect the marks from one edge to the opposite edge to make triangle shapes with a 1" base as shown in Figure 4.

4. Using a long, knotted, doubled thread, bring the needle to the front of the strip at the first mark. Stitch on the marked line to the opposite side of the strip with a long basting stitch; turn and stitch on the marked line back to opposite side as shown in Figure 5.

Figure 5

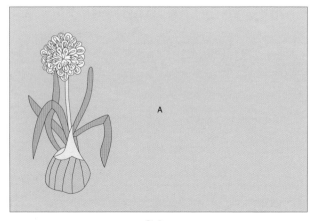

Onion
Placement Diagram 17½" x 11½"

5. Pull on the thread to gather about every 6" as shown in Figure 6. Continue to stitch and gather along the length of the strip. When you reach the end of the strip, bring needle to back of strip on top edge; take several small stitches in one place to tie off. Fold raw end to back of strip and stitch in place.

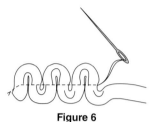

Figure 6

6. Using a new piece of knotted thread, baste one edge of the first five or six petals and pull to gather into a circle for the flower center as shown in Figure 7; knot the thread, but do not cut it.

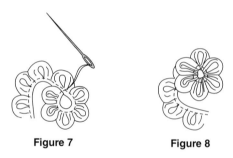

Figure 7   **Figure 8**

7. Move the gathered tail of the strip from the front to the back of the flower as shown in Figure 8; insert the needle through the flower center to move it to the back side.

8. Circle the tail around the center of the flower, stitching on the back of the flower to hold in place as you go until you reach the end of the tail to finish the flower.

9. Using 2 strands of green embroidery floss, stitch a French knot in the center of each flower petal referring to the pattern for positioning. Using 2 strands of gold embroidery floss, stem-stitch details on the onion.

10. Pin and hand-stitch the finished ruched flower at the top of the center stem piece to complete the appliqué.

Completing the Place Mat

1. Mark a 2" diagonal grid across appliquéd top using a washable fabric marker and ruler and referring to General Instructions.

2. Sandwich the 18" x 12" piece of pre-washed flannel or lightweight batting between the appliquéd A rectangle and the B rectangle.

3. Machine-quilt on the marked grid lines and close to the edges of the appliqué motifs.

4. When quilting is complete, remove marked lines.

5. Bind with white with blue dots strips following steps 3–7 in Finishing Your Quilt on page 5. ●

The onion is an underground bulb of the plant allium cepa. There are many types of onions with different-colored skins and sizes.

The name "onion," derived through the French from the Latin word "unus," meaning one. The onion is a member of the lily family, which includes the tulip, hyacinth and lily of the valley, as well as the edible leek, garlic, chive and shallot.

In the 4th century B.C., the Egyptians building the gigantic Great Pyramid were fed onions, garlic and radishes. The children of Israel cried bitterly after leaving Egypt when they were deprived of their delicacies.

The ancient Greeks and Romans used onions medicinally as well as in cooking.

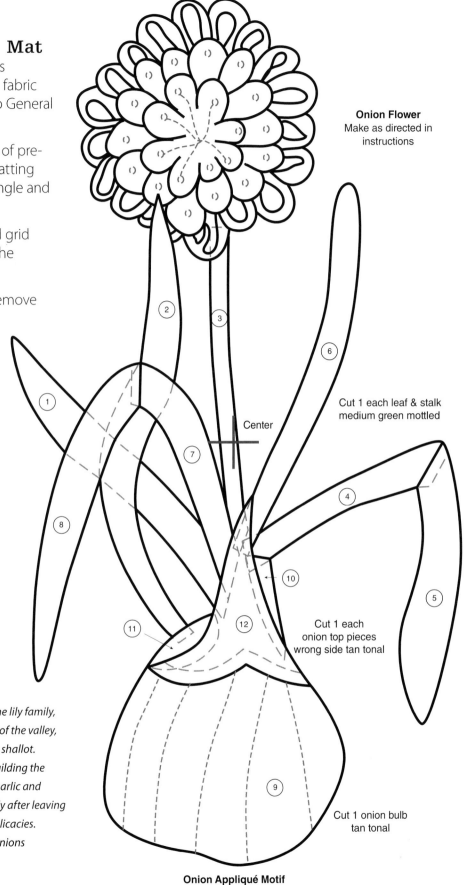

Onion Flower
Make as directed in instructions

Center

Cut 1 each leaf & stalk medium green mottled

Cut 1 each onion top pieces wrong side tan tonal

Cut 1 onion bulb tan tonal

Onion Appliqué Motif

Garlic

We remember the fish which we ate freely in Egypt, the cucumbers, the melons, the leeks, the onions, and the garlic; but now our whole being is dried up; there is nothing at all except this manna before our eyes!

—Numbers 11:5-6

Project Specifications
Place Mat Size: 17½" x 11½"

Materials
- Scraps gray/green/cream, medium green and light green mottleds
- ¼ yard white-with-blue dots
- ½ yard ⅛" blue-and-white gingham
- ½ yard ¼" blue-and-white gingham
- 18" x 12" rectangle pre-washed flannel or lightweight batting
- All-purpose thread to match fabrics
- Quilting thread
- Light green embroidery floss
- Water-erasable marker or chalk pencil
- Fabric glue stick
- Basic sewing tools and supplies

Cutting
1. Cut one 12" x 18" rectangle each ⅛" (A) and ¼" (B) blue-and-white gingham.

2. Lightly trace shapes onto the right side of the fabric as directed on pieces for color, adding extra at any areas that will be tucked under another piece.

3. Cut out shapes, adding ⅛"–¼" seam allowance all around for turning edges under.

4. Cut two 2¼" by fabric width strips white-with-blue dots for binding.

Completing the Appliqué
1. Turn edges of appliqué pieces under along tracing lines; thread- or glue-baste to hold edges in place.

2. Referring to the Placement Diagram and the full-size pattern, arrange the pieces in numerical order on the right side of A, at least ½" from the side and bottom edges of the left end; glue-baste to hold in place.

3. Hand-stitch edges of pieces in place using thread to match fabrics.

4. Using 2 strands of light green embroidery floss, stem-stitch the lines from the garlic stalk to the leaves, again referring to the appliqué motif for placement.

Completing the Place Mat
1. Mark a 2" diagonal grid across appliquéd top using a washable fabric marker and ruler and referring to General Instructions.

2. Sandwich the 18" x 12" piece of pre-washed flannel or lightweight batting between the appliquéd A rectangle and the B rectangle.

3. Machine-quilt on the marked grid lines and close to the edges of the appliqué motifs.

4. When quilting is complete, remove marked lines.

5. Bind with white-with-blue dots strips following steps 3–7 in Finishing Your Quilt on page 5. ●

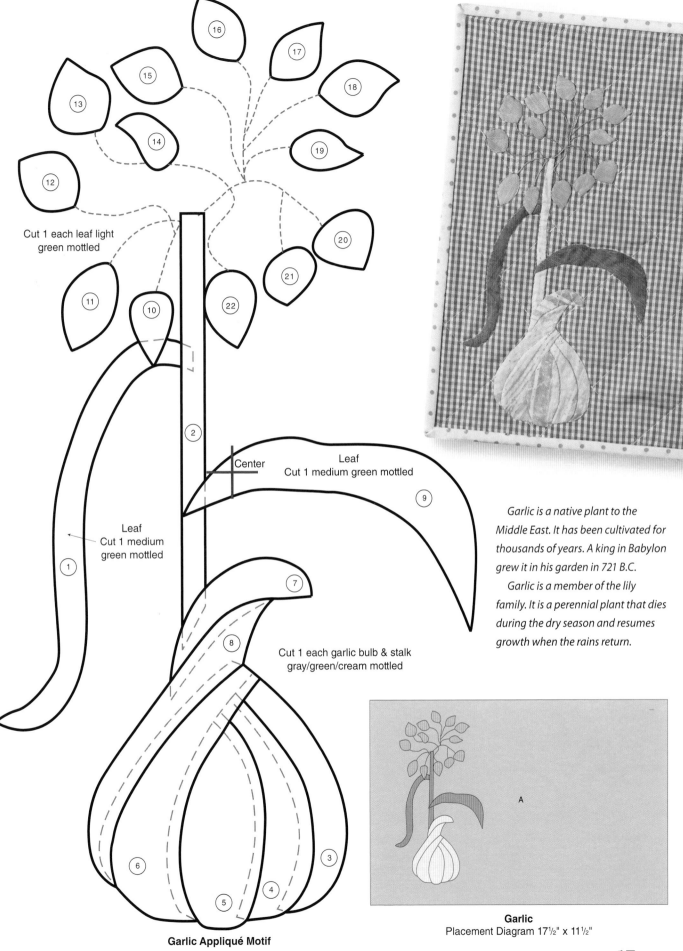

Cut 1 each leaf light green mottled

Leaf
Cut 1 medium green mottled

Center

Leaf
Cut 1 medium green mottled

Leaf
Cut 1 medium green mottled

Cut 1 each garlic bulb & stalk gray/green/cream mottled

Garlic Appliqué Motif

Garlic is a native plant to the Middle East. It has been cultivated for thousands of years. A king in Babylon grew it in his garden in 721 B.C.

Garlic is a member of the lily family. It is a perennial plant that dies during the dry season and resumes growth when the rains return.

Garlic
Placement Diagram 17½" x 11½"

A

Leek

We remember the fish which we ate freely in Egypt, the cucumbers, the melons, the leeks, the onions, and the garlic; but now our whole being is dried up; there is nothing at all except this manna before our eyes!

—Numbers 11:5-6

Project Specifications
Place Mat Size: 17½" x 11½"

Materials
- Scraps cream mottled
- Fat quarter green mottled
- ¼ yard white-with-blue dots
- ½ yard ⅛" blue-and-white gingham
- ½ yard ¼" blue-and-white gingham
- 18" x 12" rectangle pre-washed flannel or lightweight batting
- All-purpose thread to match fabrics
- Quilting thread
- Water-erasable marker or chalk pencil
- Fabric glue stick
- Basic sewing tools and supplies

Cutting
1. Cut one 12" x 18" rectangle each ⅛" (A) and ¼" (B) blue-and-white gingham.

2. Lightly trace shapes onto the right side of the fabric as directed on pieces for color, adding extra at any areas that will be tucked under another piece.

3. Cut out shapes, adding ⅛"–¼" seam allowance all around for turning edges under.

4. Cut two 2¼" by fabric width strips white-with-blue dots for binding.

Completing the Appliqué
1. Turn edges of appliqué pieces under along tracing lines; thread- or glue-baste to hold edges in place.

2. Referring to the Placement Diagram and the full-size pattern, arrange the pieces in numerical order on the right side of A, at least ½" from the side and bottom edges of the left end; glue-baste to hold in place.

3. Hand-stitch edges of pieces in place using thread to match fabrics.

Completing the Place Mat
1. Mark a 2" diagonal grid across appliquéd top using a washable fabric marker and ruler and referring to General Instructions.

2. Sandwich the 18" x 12" piece of pre-washed flannel or lightweight batting between the appliquéd A rectangle and the B rectangle.

3. Machine-quilt on the marked grid lines and close to the edges of the appliqué motifs.

4. When quilting is complete, remove marked lines.

5. Bind with white-with-blue dots strips, following steps 3–7 in Finishing Your Quilt on page 5. ●

Leek
Placement Diagram 17½" x 11½"

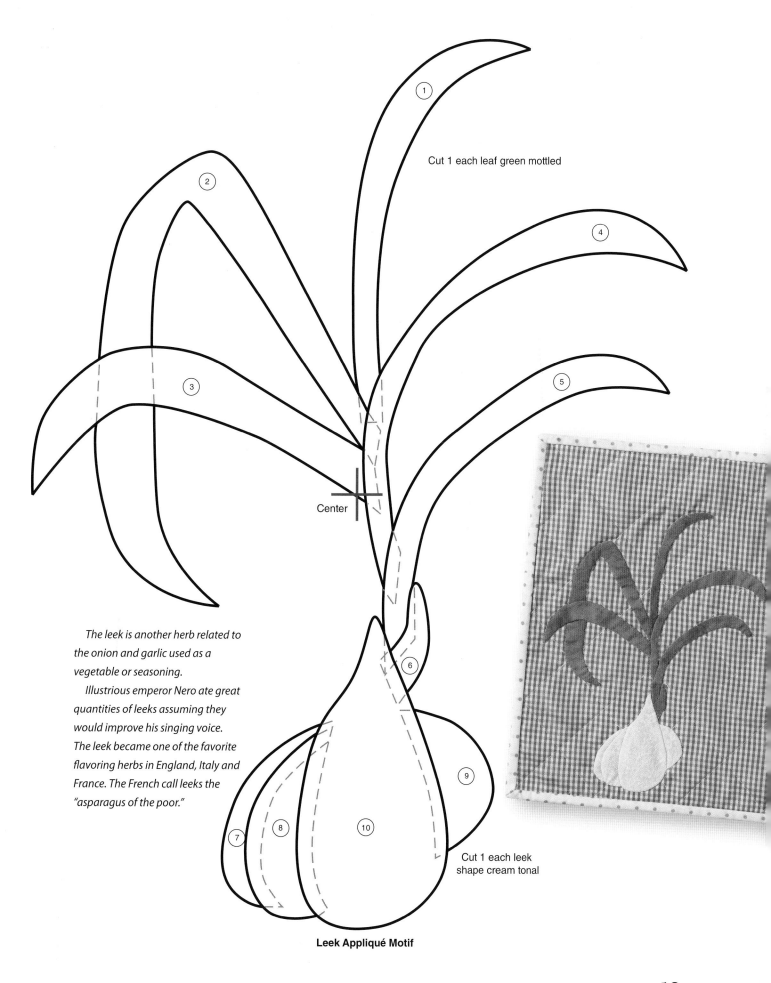

①

Cut 1 each leaf green mottled

②

④

③

⑤

Center

⑥

The leek is another herb related to the onion and garlic used as a vegetable or seasoning.

Illustrious emperor Nero ate great quantities of leeks assuming they would improve his singing voice. The leek became one of the favorite flavoring herbs in England, Italy and France. The French call leeks the "asparagus of the poor."

⑨

⑦ ⑧ ⑩

Cut 1 each leek
shape cream tonal

Leek Appliqué Motif

Shallot

We remember the fish which we ate freely in Egypt, the cucumbers, the melons, the leeks, the onions, and the garlic; but now our whole being is dried up; there is nothing at all except this manna before our eyes!

—Numbers 11:5-6

Project Specifications
Place Mat Size: 17½" x 11½"

Materials
- Scraps burgundy solid and purple mottled
- Fat quarter dark green print
- ¼ yard white-with-blue dots
- ½ yard ⅛" blue-and-white gingham
- ½ yard ¼" blue-and-white gingham
- 18" x 12" rectangle pre-washed flannel or lightweight batting
- All-purpose thread to match fabrics
- Quilting thread
- Water-erasable marker or chalk pencil
- Fabric glue stick
- Basic sewing tools and supplies

Cutting
1. Cut one 12" x 18" rectangle each ⅛" (A) and ¼" (B) blue-and-white gingham.

2. Referring to the General Instructions, prepare templates for individual appliqué shapes. Lightly trace shapes onto the right side of the fabric as directed on pieces for color, adding extra at any areas that will be tucked under another piece.

3. Cut out shapes, adding ⅛"–¼" seam allowance all around for turning edges under.

4. Cut two 2¼" by fabric width strips white-with-blue dots for binding.

Completing the Appliqué
1. Turn edges of appliqué pieces under along tracing lines; thread- or glue-baste to hold edges in place.

2. Referring to the Placement Diagram and the full-size pattern, arrange the pieces in numerical order on the right side of A, at least ½" from the side and bottom edges of the left end; glue-baste to hold in place.

3. Hand-stitch edges of pieces in place using thread to match fabrics.

Completing the Place Mat
1. Mark a 2" diagonal grid across appliquéd top using a washable fabric marker and ruler and referring to General Instructions.

2. Sandwich the 18" x 12" piece of pre-washed flannel or lightweight batting between the appliquéd A rectangle and the B rectangle.

3. Machine-quilt on the marked grid lines and close to the edges of the appliqué motifs.

4. When quilting is complete, remove marked lines.

5. Bind with the white-with-blue dots strips following steps 3–7 in Finishing Your Quilt on page 5. ●

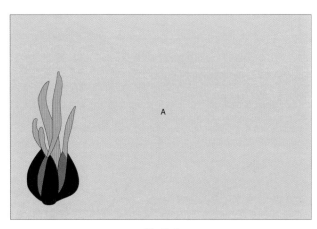

Shallot
Placement Diagram 17½" x 11½"

Herbs, Spices & Fruits of the Bible

The shallot, an herb, is a relative of the onion but has a sweeter, milder taste. It was often used in French cooking. It was believed to have been named for the ancient Israeli city, Ashkelon. Since no shallot has ever been found growing wild in fields, it is assumed to be a cultivated herb.

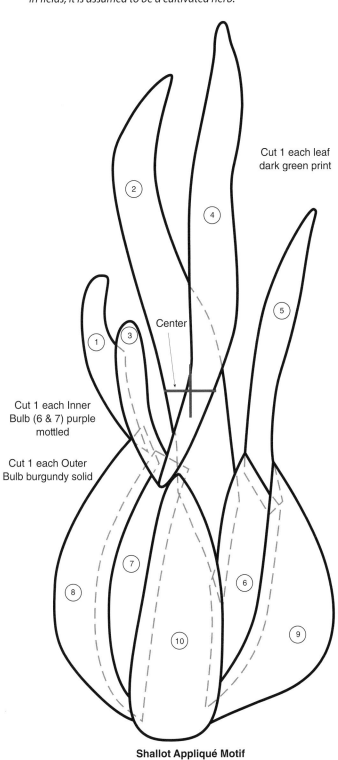

Cut 1 each leaf
dark green print

Center

Cut 1 each Inner
Bulb (6 & 7) purple
mottled

Cut 1 each Outer
Bulb burgundy solid

Shallot Appliqué Motif

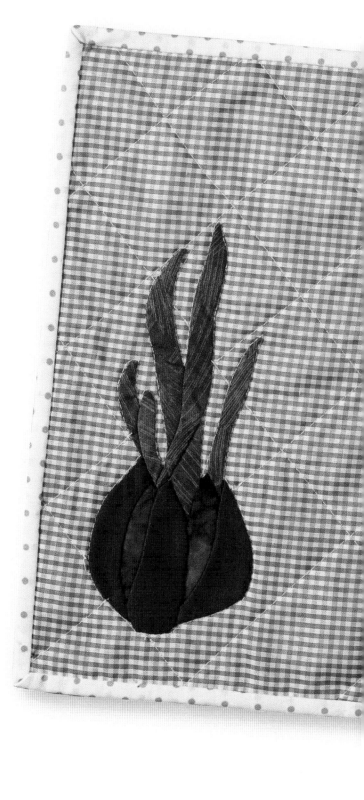

Cinnamon

I have perfumed my bed with myrrh, aloes, and cinnamon.

—Proverbs 7:17

Project Specifications
Quilt Size: 18" x 18"

Materials
- Fat quarter yellow tonal
- Fat quarter green leaf print
- Fat quarter red mottled
- Fat quarter red/green print
- ¼ yard green print
- ⅝ yard cream mottled
- Batting 22" x 22"
- Backing 22" x 22"
- All-purpose thread to match fabrics
- Quilting thread
- Green embroidery floss
- Water-erasable marker or chalk pencil
- Fabric glue stick
- ¼" bias bar
- Basic sewing tools and supplies

Cinnamon
Placement Diagram 18" x 18"

Cutting
1. Cut one 14½" x 14½" A square cream mottled.

2. Cut 13 yellow tonal yo-yo circles using pattern given.

3. Cut and piece bias strips and join, if necessary to make two 1" x 15" bias strips red mottled.

4. Cut two 2½" x 14½" B strips and two 2½" x 18½" C strips red/green print.

5. Lightly trace each individual leaf shape onto the right side of the green leaf print, adding extra at any areas that will be tucked under another piece.

6. Cut out shapes, adding ⅛"–¼" seam allowance all around for turning edges under.

7. Cut two 2¼" by fabric width strips green print for binding.

Making Yo-yos
1. Thread a needle and knot the end.

2. Working with the wrong side of the fabric toward you, insert the needle in the edge of the fabric on the wrong side so the knot will be inside the yo-yo as shown in Figure 1.

Figure 1

3. Sew a basic running stitch around the edge of the circle, turning the edge under as you sew as shown in Figure 2. Stop when you reach the starting point.

Figure 2

4. Hold the needle and pull the thread to gather the circle as shown in Figure 3.

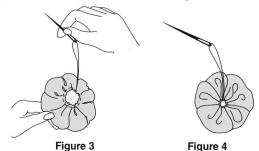

Figure 3   **Figure 4**

5. Tuck the edge into the center, keeping the right side of the fabric out as you gather the fabric as shown in Figure 4.

6. Gather until you have an almost-closed circle as shown in Figure 5.

Figure 5   **Figure 6**

7. While holding close to the fabric so the gathers do not slip, knot the thread multiple times; trim the threads close to the knots.

8. Finger-press the yo-yo flat with the hole in the center to finish as shown in Figure 6.

Completing the Appliqué

1. Fold the A square horizontally and vertically and crease to mark the center.

2. Fold bias strips along length with wrong sides together; stitch along long raw edges. Trim seam to ⅛"; insert the ¼" bias bar, center seam and press open.

3. Using the full-size pattern as a guide for positioning, center and create the arch; glue-baste in place.

4. Cut shorter pieces and insert under the glued arch referring to pattern for positioning; glue-baste to hold in place.

5. Hand-stitch the arch and shorter pieces in place using matching thread.

6. Turn edges of leaf shapes under along tracing lines; thread- or glue-baste to hold edges in place.

7. Referring to the Placement Diagram and the full-size pattern, arrange the leaves on the red arch and at the end of the shorter red pieces; glue-baste, then hand-stitch in place using thread to match leaf fabric.

8. Arrange the stitched yo-yos at the ends of the short red bias pieces with the gathered side down referring to the Placement Diagram and full-size pattern for positioning.

9. Using 1 strand green embroidery floss, stem-stitch detail lines onto all leaves referring to the appliqué patterns for color and positioning.

Completing the Quilt

1. Sew a B strip to opposite sides and C strips to the top and bottom of the appliquéd A square; press seams toward A and B strips.

2. Layer, quilt and bind referring to Finishing Your Quilt on page 5. ●

The reddish-brown spice comes from the dried bark of the shrub-like Evergreen trees of the cinnamon family, which belong to the Laurel group. This is one of the spices that is not obtained from seeds, flowers or fruits.

Cinnamon is a native of Sri Lanka. People in the Old Testament valued cinnamon highly as a spice perfume and a chief ingredient of holy oil.

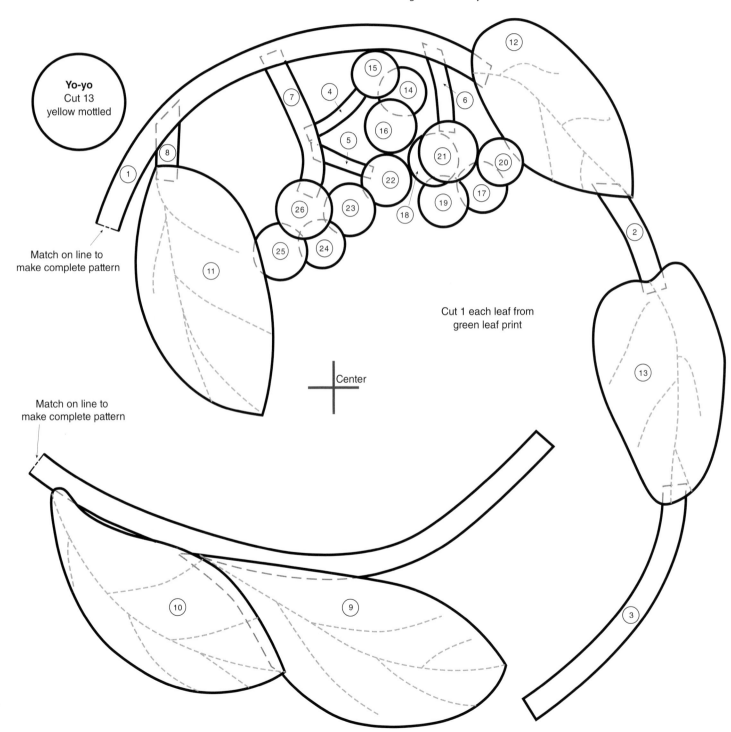

Yo-yo
Cut 13
yellow mottled

Match on line to make complete pattern

Match on line to make complete pattern

Cut 1 each leaf from green leaf print

Center

Saffron

Spikenard and saffron, Calamus and cinnamon, With all trees of frankincense, Myrrh and aloes, With all chief spices.

—Song of Solomon: 4:14

The crocus we grow in our gardens today is slightly different from the Biblical variety. The saffron crocus provided seasoning, yellow dye, incense and medicine obtained from the three stigmas. It is the most expensive spice because it takes 4,300 flowers to make one ounce of saffron. Mixed with oil, the aromatic product also served as a condiment, a perfume and medicine.

Project Specifications
Quilt Size: 12½" x 16½"

Materials
- Scrap purple mottled
- Scraps yellow, pale green, medium purple and red solids
- Scrap cream/green mottled
- Fat eighth lavender solid
- Fat eight brown mottled
- Fat quarter green solid
- Fat quarter light blue mottled
- ¼ yard white/blue mottled
- Batting 16" x 20"
- Backing 16" x 20"
- All-purpose thread to match fabrics
- Quilting thread
- Brown, purple, lavender, medium green and pale green embroidery floss
- Water-erasable marker or chalk pencil
- Fabric glue stick
- Basic sewing tools and supplies

Cutting
1. Cut one 7" x 20½" A rectangle and two 3½" x 20½" B rectangles light blue mottled.

2. Cut and piece bias strips and join to make a ¾" x 50" bias strip green solid for the narrow leaves.

3. Lightly trace each individual shape (except the narrow leaves) onto the right side of the fabrics as directed on pattern for color, adding extra at any areas that will be tucked under another piece.

4. Cut out shapes, adding ⅛"–¼" seam allowance all around for turning edges under.

5. Cut two 2¼" by fabric width strips white/blue mottled for binding.

Completing the Background

1. Sew B to each side of A as shown in Figure 1; press seams toward B.

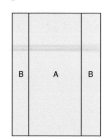

Figure 1

2. Fold the A-B unit along the length and crease to mark the center; unfold.

3. Measure up 3¾" on each long side and make a mark referring to Figure 2.

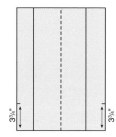

Figure 2

4. Using a straightedge, draw a line from the side marks to the center crease as shown in Figure 3; trim along the marked line to complete A-B background, again referring to Figure 3.

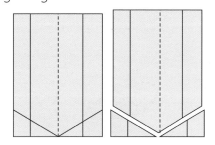

Figure 3

Completing the Appliqué

1. Fold the A-B unit horizontally and vertically and crease to mark the center.

2. Turn edges of appliqué shapes under along tracing lines; thread- or glue-baste to hold edges in place.

3. Turn edges of the bias strip to the wrong side, overlapping as necessary to make a ⅛"-wide strip; glue-baste down the center to hold edges in place. Cut the baste strip into pieces as needed for appliqué. Fold the exposed end under and glue-baste in place.

4. Referring to the Placement Diagram and the full-size pattern, arrange the pieces in place on center of the A-B background, overlapping as necessary; glue-baste then hand-stitch in place using thread to match fabrics.

Completing the Quilt

1. Using 1 strand of embroidery floss and a stem stitch, stitch the embroidered lines as marked on the pattern for positioning and color, including close to the edges of several areas as shown in Figure 4.

Figure 4

2. Layer, quilt and bind referring to Finishing Your Quilt on page 5. ●

Saffron
Placement Diagram 12½" x 16½"

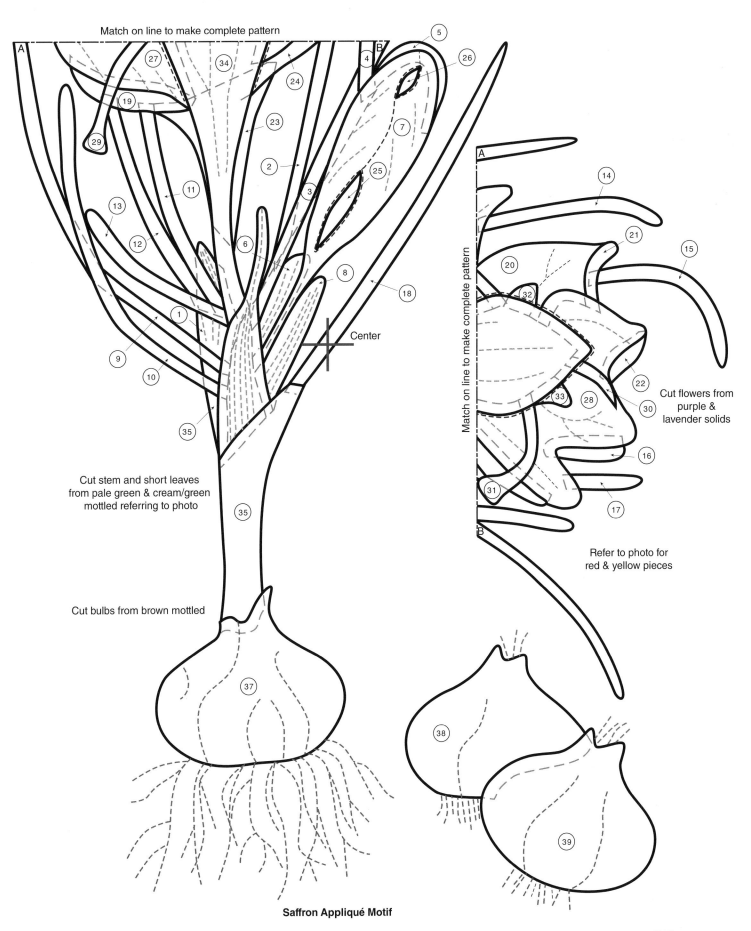

Match on line to make complete pattern

Match on line to make complete pattern

Center

Cut flowers from
purple &
lavender solids

Cut stem and short leaves
from pale green & cream/green
mottled referring to photo

Refer to photo for
red & yellow pieces

Cut bulbs from brown mottled

Saffron Appliqué Motif

Mint

But woe to you Pharisees! For you tithe mint and rue and all manner of herbs, and pass by justice and the love of God. These you ought to have done, without leaving the others undone.

—Luke 11:42

Project Specifications
Quilt Size: 18" x 18"
Block Size: 13" x 13"

Materials
- Fat quarter medium green tonal
- Fat quarter tan tonal
- Fat quarter cream floral
- Fat quarter medium green leaf tonal
- Fat quarter cream batik
- ¼ yard green print
- Batting 22" x 22"
- Backing 22" x 22"
- All-purpose thread to match fabrics
- Quilting thread
- Red and light green embroidery floss
- Water-erasable marker or chalk pencil
- Fabric glue stick
- Basic sewing tools and supplies

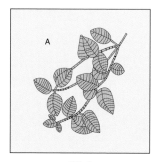

Mint
13" x 13" Block
Make 1

Cutting
1. Cut one 13½" x 13½" A square cream batik.

2. Cut four 13½" x 3" B strips green leaf tonal.

3. Cut four 3" x 3" C squares cream floral.

4. Cut two 2½" by fabric width strips green print for binding.

5. Lightly trace each individual appliqué shape onto the right side of the fabrics as directed on pattern for color, adding extra at any areas that will be tucked under another piece.

6. Cut out shapes, adding ⅛"–¼" seam allowance all around for turning edges under.

Completing the Appliqué
1. Fold the A square horizontally and vertically and crease to mark the centers.

2. Turn edges of the appliqué shapes under along tracing lines; thread- or glue-baste to hold edges in place.

3. Referring to the block drawing and the full-size pattern, arrange the pieces in place on the center of the A background square, overlapping as necessary; glue-baste then hand-stitch in place using thread to match fabrics.

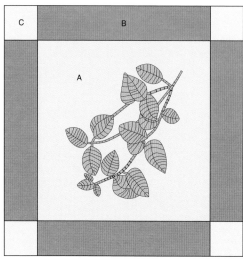

Mint
Placement Diagram 18" x 18"

Mint is native to the Middle East where it is used for flavoring in many dishes.

According to the Bible, mint was considered a religious tithe to God. The Jews ate mint with their pascal lamb.

Mint can be found growing wild near springs or rivers but also is a garden herb. Today mint is used in chewing gum, candies, medicine, vegetable dishes, juleps and tea.

4. Use 1 strand of red embroidery floss and a straight stitch to add lines to the plant stem.

5. Use 2 strands of embroidery floss and a stem stitch to add detail lines as marked on all mint leaves, referring to each of the full-size motifs for positioning and color placement.

Completing the Top

1. Sew a B strip to opposite sides of the stitched block; press seams toward B strips.

2. Sew a C square to each end of each remaining B strip; press seams toward B.

3. Sew a B-C strip to the remaining sides of the stitched block; press seams toward the B-C strips to complete the top.

Completing the Quilt

1. Layer, quilt and bind referring to Finishing Your Quilt on page 5. ●

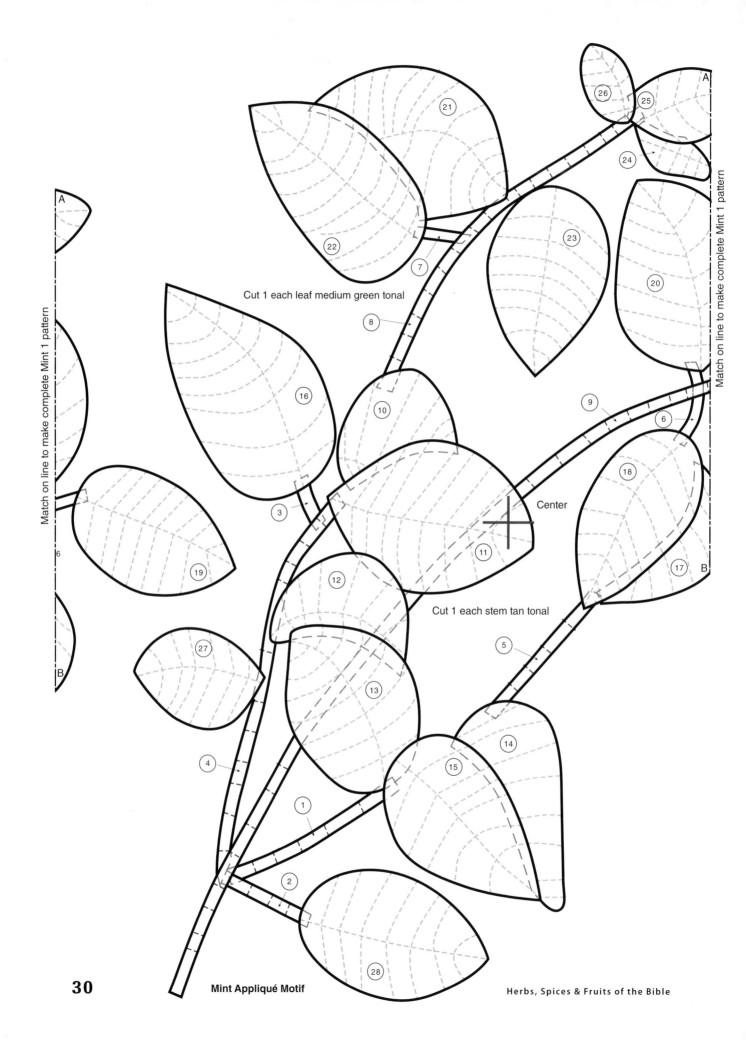

Cut 1 each leaf medium green tonal

Center

Cut 1 each stem tan tonal

Mint Appliqué Motif

Cumin

Woe to you, scribes and Pharisees, hypocrites! For you pay tithe of mint and anise and cummin, and have neglected the weightier matters of the law: justice and mercy and faith. These you ought to have done, without leaving the others undone.

—Matthew 23:23

Project Specifications
Quilt Size: 17" x 17"

Materials
- Scraps 1 dark, 1 medium and 2 light teal solids
- Fat eighth dark brown mottled
- Fat quarter each medium teal tonal, cream mottled and light teal print
- ¼ yard brown solid
- Batting 21" x 21"
- Backing 21" x 21"
- All-purpose thread to match fabrics
- Quilting thread
- Black and light teal embroidery floss
- Water-erasable marker or chalk pencil
- Fabric glue stick
- Basic sewing tools and supplies

Cutting
1. Cut one 14½" x 14½" A square cream mottled.

2. Cut two 2" x 14½" B strips and two 2" x 17½" C strips light teal print.

3. Lightly trace each individual shape onto the right side of the fabrics as directed on pattern for color, adding extra at any areas that will be tucked under another piece.

4. Cut out shapes, adding ⅛"–¼" seam allowance all around for turning edges under.

5. Cut two 2¼" by fabric width strips brown solid for binding.

Completing the Appliqué
1. Fold the A square horizontally and vertically and crease to mark the center.

2. Turn edges of appliqué shapes under along tracing lines; thread- or glue-baste to hold in place.

3. Referring to the Placement Diagram and the full-size pattern, arrange the pieces in place on center of the A background, overlapping as necessary; glue-baste then hand-stitch in place using thread to match fabrics.

Completing the Quilt
1. Using 1 strand of teal embroidery floss and a stem stitch, outline-stitch around the base of the flower and as desired.

2. Outline around each dark brown petal using 1 strand of black embroidery floss and a stem stitch.

3. Sew a B strip to opposite sides and C strips to the top and bottom of the stitched center; press seams toward B and C strips.

4. Layer, quilt and bind referring to Finishing Your Quilt on page 5. ●

Cut 1 each medium teal tonal

Cut 1 medium teal tonal

Cut 1 dark teal solid

Match on line to make complete pattern

Center

Cumin Appliqué Motif

Cumin
Placement Diagram 17" x 17"

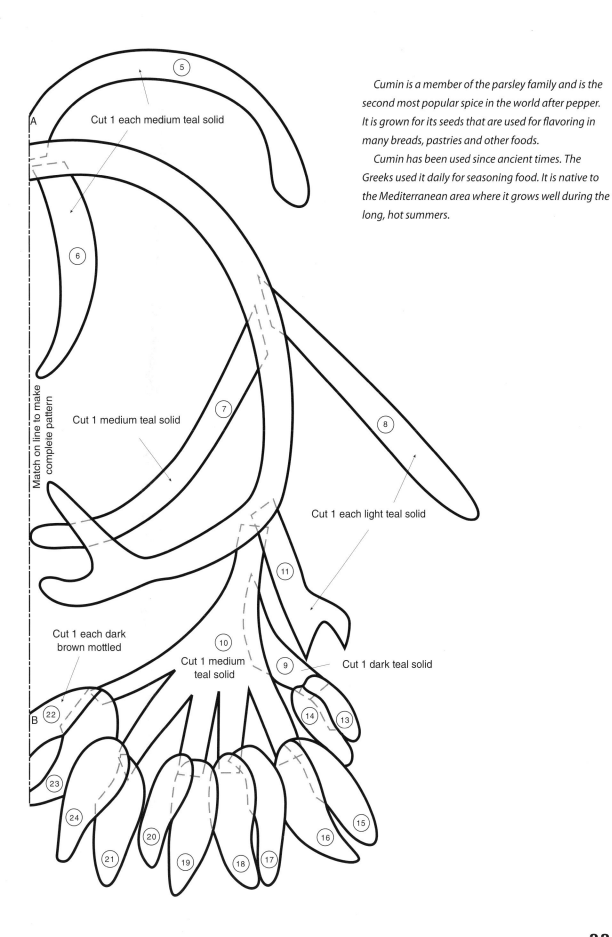

Cut 1 each medium teal solid

Match on line to make complete pattern

Cut 1 medium teal solid

Cut 1 each light teal solid

Cut 1 each dark brown mottled

Cut 1 medium teal solid

Cut 1 dark teal solid

A

B

5

6

7

8

11

10

9

14

13

22

23

24

20

21

19

18

17

16

15

Cumin is a member of the parsley family and is the second most popular spice in the world after pepper. It is grown for its seeds that are used for flavoring in many breads, pastries and other foods.

Cumin has been used since ancient times. The Greeks used it daily for seasoning food. It is native to the Mediterranean area where it grows well during the long, hot summers.

Mustard

So Jesus said to them, … if you have faith as a mustard seed, you will say to this mountain, 'Move from here to there,' and it will move; and nothing will be impossible for you.

—Matthew 17:20

There are several species of mustard plants, some of which have very small seeds. They germinate and grow quickly. Some species can grow to a height of 10–12 feet, much larger than other types of herbs.

The seeds can be used as a spice, or ground and mixed with other ingredients into a condiment. The leaves of the mustard plant are also edible.

Project Notes

The wreath and some of the leaves on this project were fused rather than hand-appliquéd in place. Because this quilt probably won't require repeated laundering, the fused pieces have not been edge-stitched.

Project Specifications

Quilt Size: 15" x 15"

Materials

- Scraps 3 different teal tonals or mottleds and white solid
- Fat quarter medium teal and cream mottleds
- Fat quarter yellow solid
- Fat quarter coordinating stripe with ⅝"-wide repeating design
- Batting 19" x 19"
- Backing 19" x 19"
- All-purpose thread to match fabrics
- Quilting thread
- Bright and light olive green embroidery floss
- Water-erasable marker or chalk pencil
- Fabric glue stick
- 1 small bumblebee button
- Basic sewing tools and supplies

Cutting

1. Cut one 13½" x 13½" A square cream mottled.

2. Cut four 1½" by 21" strips yellow solid; subcut strips into two 13½" B strips and two 15½" C strips.

3. Prepare fusible web templates, following guidelines under Machine Appliqué in the General Instructions on page 4, for the one-piece wreath 6 and stem 5 and leaves 1–4, 7 and 9–14. **Note:** *The ring around the outside and the stem through the center are all one piece when cutting and stitching.*

4. Again referring to General Instructions, prepare templates for leaf appliqué shapes 8 and 15–21. Lightly trace shapes onto the right side of the fabrics as directed on pattern for color and cut out.

5. Prepare a template for the flower circle using the pattern given.

6. Cut four 2¼" x 18" binding strips, centering the repeating design of the stripe in each strip.

Completing the Appliqué

1. Fold the A square horizontally and vertically and crease to mark the center.

2. Turn edges of leaf 8 and 15–21 appliqué shapes under along tracing lines; thread- or glue-baste to hold edges in place.

3. Referring to the Placement Diagram and the full-size pattern, arrange the pieces in place on center of the A background, overlapping as necessary; glue-baste leaf 8 and 15–21 and apply fusible-web pieces in ascending order. Hand-stitch glue-basted pieces in place using thread to match fabrics.

4. Using 1 strand light olive embroidery floss, stem-stitch leaves as marked on appliqué pattern.

Completing the Flowers

1. Trace 14 circle shapes onto the wrong side of the yellow solid, leaving at least ½" between pieces.

2. Layer the traced section of fabric right sides together with a same-size piece of yellow solid; pin through each traced circle to hold.

3. Cut out shapes through the two layers, leaving the layers pinned together.

4. To make one flower, using a knotted double thread, sew a running stitch ¼" from edge all around; knot the end and cut, but do not gather the thread.

5. Carefully cut a small X in the center of one of the circle layers as shown in Figure 1; turn the circle right side out through the slits.

Figure 1   **Figure 2**

6. Fold the circle in half and crease; unfold and fold in half again and crease. Using a water-erasable marker, mark a dot at the edges of the creased lines as shown in Figure 2.

7. With a doubled knotted thread, come up through the center of the circle; wrap the thread over the mark at the top of the circle and bring the needle up again at the center as shown in Figure 3.

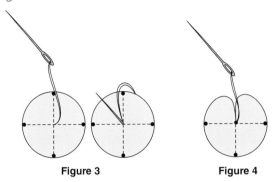

Figure 3   **Figure 4**

8. Pull the thread up tight and knot as shown in Figure 4; do not cut the thread.

9. Repeat steps 7 and 8 at each mark on the edge of the circle in a clockwise direction to create a four-petal flower as shown in Figure 5.

Figure 5

10. Repeat steps 4–9 to complete a total of 14 yellow flowers.

Mustard
Placement Diagram 15" x 15"

11. Repeat steps 1–9 with white solid to make just one white flower.

12. Using 2 strands bright green embroidery floss, make a French knot in the center of each flower.

Completing the Quilt

1. Sew a B strip to opposite sides and C strips to the top and bottom of the stitched center; press seams toward B and C strips.

2. Layer, quilt and bind referring to Finishing Your Quilt on page 5.

3. Arrange and tack the flowers on the completed quilt top referring to the pattern for positioning.

4. Stitch the bumblebee button in place at the edge of the flowers to finish. ●

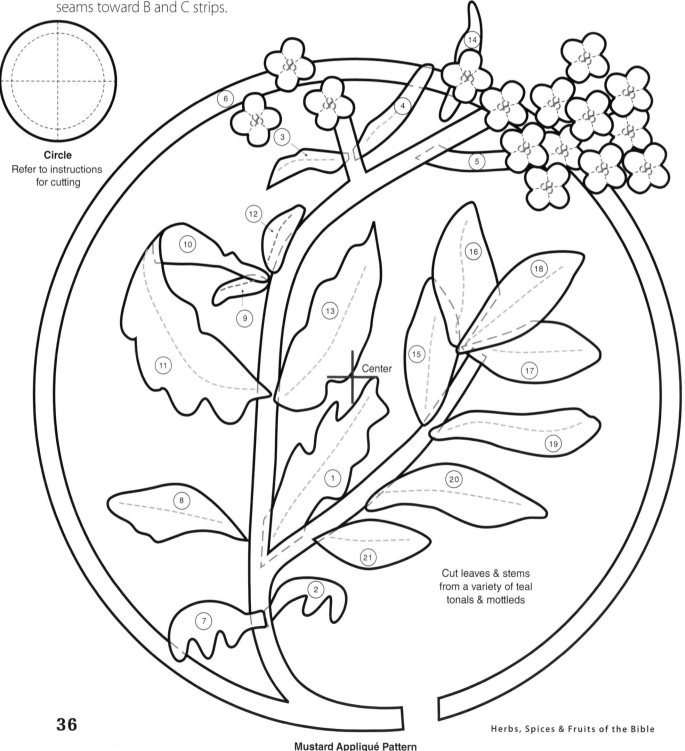

Circle
Refer to instructions for cutting

Center

Cut leaves & stems from a variety of teal tonals & mottleds

Olives

You prepare a table before me in the presence of my enemies; You anoint my head with oil; My cup runs over.

—Psalms 23:5

Project Note

This olive block along with the Figs, Grapes and Dates blocks that follow (see pages 40–44) when set together create a unique Fruits of the Bible quilt. Instructions for this quilt are found on page 39.

Olive Block

Project Specifications

Block Size: 13" x 13"
Number of Blocks: 1

Materials

- Scraps medium and dark green and dark brown tonals
- 13½" x 13½" A square cream tonal
- All-purpose thread to match fabrics
- Quilting thread
- Medium green embroidery floss
- Water-erasable marker or chalk pencil
- Fabric glue stick
- Basic sewing tools and supplies

Cutting

1. Lightly trace each individual appliqué shape onto the right side of the fabrics as directed on pattern for color, adding extra at any areas that will be tucked under another piece.

2. Cut out shapes, adding ⅛"–¼" seam allowance all around for turning edges under.

Completing the Appliqué

1. Fold the A square horizontally and vertically and crease to mark the center.

2. Turn edges of appliqué shapes under along tracing lines; thread- or glue-baste to hold edges in place.

Olives
Placement Diagram
13" x 13"

3. Referring to the Placement Diagram and the full-size pattern, arrange the pieces in place on center of the A background, overlapping as necessary; glue-baste then hand-stitch in place using thread to match fabrics.

4. Using 2 strands of green embroidery floss, add detail lines as marked on pattern for color and positioning.

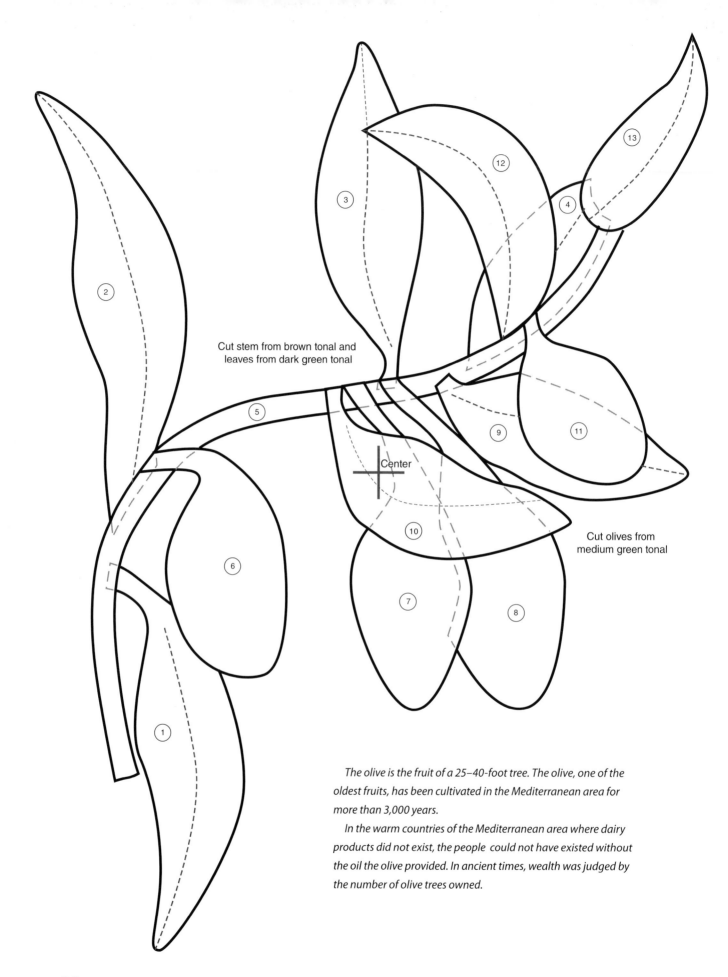

Cut stem from brown tonal and
leaves from dark green tonal

Center

Cut olives from
medium green tonal

The olive is the fruit of a 25–40-foot tree. The olive, one of the
oldest fruits, has been cultivated in the Mediterranean area for
more than 3,000 years.

In the warm countries of the Mediterranean area where dairy
products did not exist, the people could not have existed without
the oil the olive provided. In ancient times, wealth was judged by
the number of olive trees owned.

Fruits of the Bible Wall Quilt

Project Specifications

Quilt Size: 30½" x 30½"
Block Size: 13" x 13"
Number of Blocks: 4

Materials

- 4 (13½" x 13½") embroidered blocks (Olives, Dates, Figs and Grapes used in sample)
- ¾ yard green print
- Batting 35" x 35"
- Backing 35" x 35"
- All-purpose thread to match fabrics
- Quilting thread
- Basic sewing tools and supplies

Cutting

1. Cut one 2" by fabric width strip green print; subcut strip into two 13½" B strips.

2. Cut three 2" x 28" C strips and two 2" x 31" D strips green print.

3. Cut four 2¼" by fabric width strips green print for binding.

Completing the Top

1. Join two 13½" x 13½" embroidered fruit blocks with a B strip to make a vertical row; press seams toward B strips. Repeat to make a second vertical row.

2. Join the two vertical rows with a C strip; press seams toward C.

3. Sew a C strip to the top and bottom and D strips to opposite sides of the joined section to complete the quilt top.

Completing the Quilt

1. Layer, quilt and bind referring to Finishing Your Quilt on page 5. ●

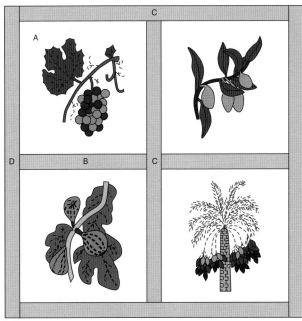

Fruit Block Wall Quilt
Placement Diagram 30½" x 30½"

Dates

The next day a great multitude that had come to the feast, when they heard that Jesus was coming to Jerusalem, took branches of palm trees and went out to meet Him, and cried out: Hosanna! Blessed is He who comes in the name of the LORD!

—John 12:12-13

Project Notes

The date shapes are fused rather than hand-appliquéd in place. Because the pieces are small, fusible appliqué would make applying them easier. Refer to Machine Appliqué fusible web application on page 4 as needed. The pieces were not stitched after fusing; depending on use, fusing without stitching is an acceptable method.

Project Specifications

Block Size: 13" x 13"
Number of Blocks: 1

Materials

- Scraps burgundy print and light, medium and dark green prints
- Scrap dark red solid
- 13½" x 13½" A square cream tonal

Dates
Placement Diagram
13" x 13"

- All-purpose thread to match fabrics
- Quilting thread
- Brown and 2 shades of medium green embroidery floss
- Water-erasable marker or chalk pencil
- Fabric glue stick
- Basic sewing tools and supplies

Cutting

1. Lightly trace the tree trunk appliqué shape onto the right side of the fabric as directed on pattern for color.

2. Cut out shape, adding ⅛"–¼" seam allowance all around for turning edges under.

3. Prepare date shapes for fusible appliqué referring to the Project Notes.

Completing the Appliqué

1. Fold the A square horizontally and vertically and crease to mark the center.

2. Turn edges of tree trunk appliqué shape under along tracing lines; thread- or glue-baste to hold edges in place.

3. Referring to the Placement Diagram and the full-size pattern, place the tree trunk piece on the A background; glue-baste then hand-stitch in place using thread to match fabric.

4. Fuse the date shapes in place. Fuse the date shapes in place referring to full-size pattern for positioning.

5. Using 2 strands of embroidery floss and a stem stitch, add detail lines as marked on pattern for positioning and color placement.
Note: *Two close lines of stem stitches create the hanging stems that attach the dates to the tree.* ●

The date is the fruit of the date palm tree. The tree grows to 100 feet tall, often reaching 200 years of age.

The fruit of the date palm is a one-seeded berry, which grows in thick clusters. Dates can be soft, hard or dry.

The date palm is one of the oldest and most valuable of food plants with a history of over 5,000 years.

Center

Match on line to make complete pattern

Match on line to make complete pattern

Figs

…they sewed fig leaves together and made themselves coverings.

—Genesis 3:7

Project Specifications
Block Size: 13" x 13"
Number of Blocks: 1

Materials
- Scraps light terra cotta and brown/green batiks and green tonal
- 13½" x 13½" A square cream tonal
- All-purpose thread to match fabrics
- Quilting thread
- Light and medium green, medium and dark purple, and gold embroidery floss
- Water-erasable marker or chalk pencil
- Fabric glue stick
- Basic sewing tools and supplies

Cutting
1. Lightly trace each individual appliqué shape onto the right side of the fabrics as directed on pattern for color, adding extra at any areas that will be tucked under another piece.

2. Cut out shapes, adding ⅛"–¼" seam allowance all around for turning edges under.

Figs
Placement Diagram
13" x 13"

Completing the Appliqué
1. Fold the A square horizontally and vertically and crease to mark the center.

2. Turn edges of appliqué shapes under along tracing lines; thread- or glue-baste to hold edges in place.

3. Referring to the Placement Diagram and the full-size pattern, arrange the pieces in place on center of the A background, overlapping as necessary; glue-baste then hand-stitch in place using thread to match fabrics.

4. Using 2 strands of embroidery floss and a stem stitch, add detail lines on leaves and figs referring to pattern for positioning and color placement. ●

The fig is the fruit of the ficus carica. Fig trees can live up to 200 years and can produce several crops in one year. There are about 600-800 varieties varying in size and color. Some varieties are self-pollenating and produce some of the most tasty figs. Figs can easily be dried and stored for later use.

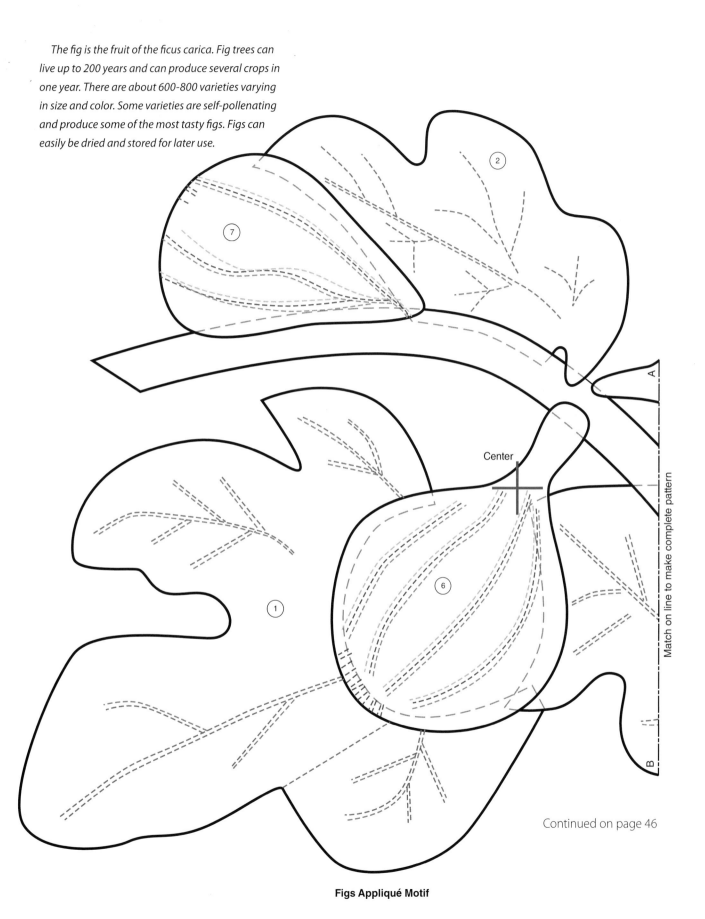

Center

Match on line to make complete pattern

Continued on page 46

Figs Appliqué Motif

Grapes

Let us get up early to the vineyards; Let us see if the vine has budded, Whether the grape blossoms are open, And the pomegranates are in bloom.

—Song of Solomon 7:12

Project Specifications
Block Size: 13" x 13"
Number of Blocks: 1

Materials
- Scraps purple batik and medium and dark green tonals
- 13½" x 13½" A square cream tonal
- All-purpose thread to match fabrics
- Quilting thread
- Light and medium green embroidery floss
- Water-erasable marker or chalk pencil
- Fabric glue stick
- Template material or cardboard
- Basic sewing tools and supplies

Cutting
1. Lightly trace each individual appliqué shape, except the grapes, onto the right side of the fabrics as directed on pattern for color, adding extra at any areas that will be tucked under another piece.

2. Cut out shapes, adding ⅛"–¼" seam allowance all around for turning edges under.

Making Grapes
1. Cut a circle piece from cardboard or template material the same size as a grape circle in the pattern.

2. Cut a fabric circle ⅛" larger than the cardboard circle. Hand-stitch all around the fabric circle ⅛" from edge.

3. Place the stitched fabric circle on the small cardboard circle; pull thread to gather fabric around cardboard. Press well around edge using the tip of the iron. Clip stitching and carefully remove cardboard; press again.

4. Repeat steps 1–3 to make a total of 26 grape circles

Completing the Appliqué
1. Fold the A square horizontally and vertically and crease to mark the center.

2. Turn edges of appliqué shapes under along tracing lines; thread- or glue-baste to hold edges in place.

3. Referring to the Placement Diagram and the full-size pattern, arrange the pieces in place on center of the A background, overlapping as necessary; glue-baste then hand-stitch in place using thread to match fabrics.

4. Using 2 strands of embroidery floss, add detail lines as marked on pattern for color and positioning. ●

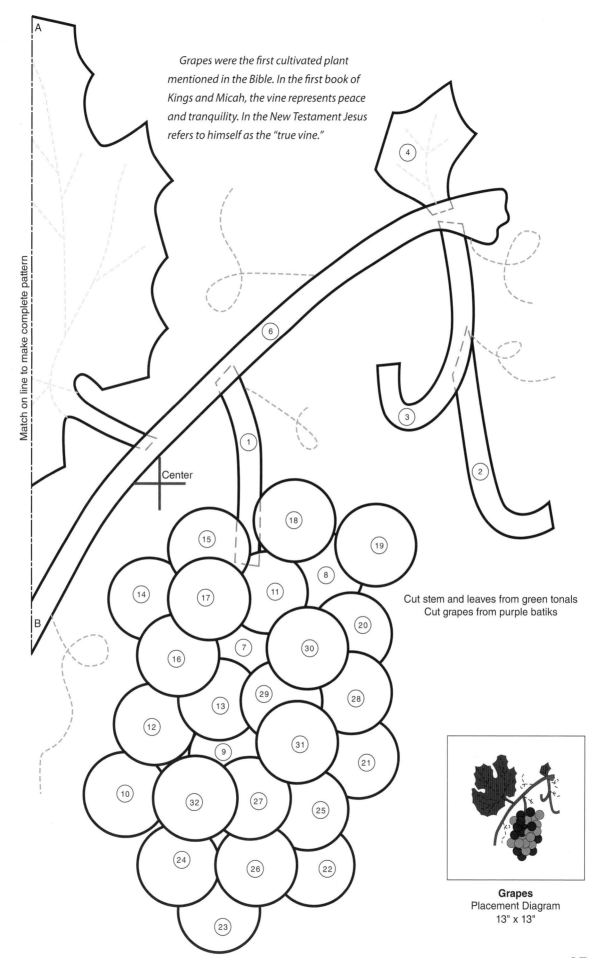

Grapes were the first cultivated plant mentioned in the Bible. In the first book of Kings and Micah, the vine represents peace and tranquility. In the New Testament Jesus refers to himself as the "true vine."

A

Match on line to make complete pattern

B

Center

Cut stem and leaves from green tonals
Cut grapes from purple batiks

Grapes
Placement Diagram
13" x 13"

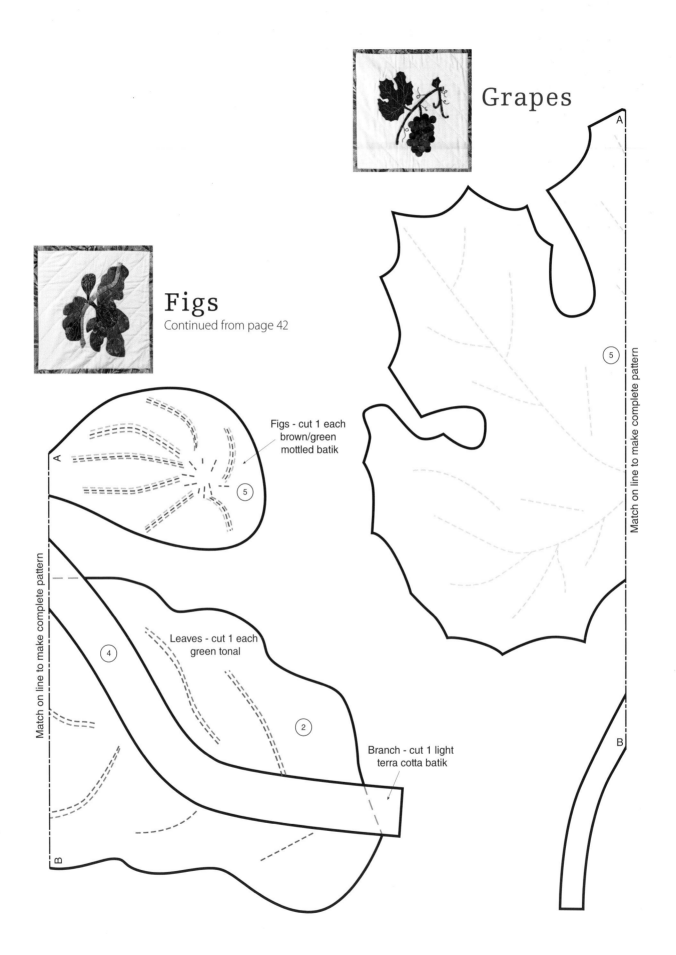

Grapes

Figs

Continued from page 42

Figs - cut 1 each
brown/green
mottled batik

⑤

A

Match on line to make complete pattern

⑤

Match on line to make complete pattern

B

Leaves - cut 1 each
green tonal

④

②

Branch - cut 1 light
terra cotta batik

A

B

Meet the Designer

Helga Curtis started her career in the arts by attending Traphagen School of Fashion and Design, Fashion Insitute of Technology and New York University in New York City. During her long and varied career, Helga has owned an art gallery and a fashion design studio, served as fund raiser and lecturer for a mental health clinic and been an instrutor of needle arts, a quilt designer and a newspaper columnist. She has served as a consultant and instructor for historical societies in New York and Georgia. In 1977 she was appointed by the federal Bicentennial Commission as a quilt coordinator. She designed and helped construct a quilt depicting Staten Island, N.Y. circa 1700-1800.

Helga moved to Florida in 1981 where she still makes her home. She continues to be active in quilt design and instruction at clubs and colleges. She has had numerous designs published in quilting magazines over the years.

Acknowledgements

Thanks to the following quilters and embroiders:
Paula Breckler, Linda Donnelly, Ann Hettel, Emily Heffren, Joyce Kenney, Carolyn Small, Lynn Squires, Marie Taverna and Robin Wood.

Scripture taken from the New King James Version. Copyright © 1982 by Thomas Nelson Inc. Used by permission. All rights reserved.

Bibliography

Wicked Plants *by Amy Stewart*

Magic and Medicine of Plants *from the editors of* Reader's Digest *books.*

Woman's Day Encyclopedia of Cookery *Volumes 1–12.*

Herbs of the Bible *by James A. Duke, Ph.D.*

Fauna and Flora of the Bible, *United Bible Societies, London.*

Plants of the Bible *by Harold N. Moldenke, Ph.D.*

Garden Section, *St. Petersburg Times, October 10, 2009.*

Get Happy with Herbs, Woman's World *April 2009 to the present.*

Mother Earth's Medicine Chest *by Yvonne Swanson.*

Where to Find It in the Bible *by Ken Anderson.*

The Clear Word Bible *by Bob and Helen Hammond.*

Herb Companion *magazine.*

Florida's Best Herbs and Spices *by Charles R. Boning.*

HOUSE of WHITE BIRCHES PUBLISHERS SINCE 1947

Herbs, Spices & Fruits of the Bible is published by DRG, 306 East Parr Road, Berne, IN 46711. Printed in USA. Copyright © 2011 DRG. All rights reserved. This publication may not be reproduced in part or in whole without written permission from the publisher.

RETAIL STORES: If you would like to carry this pattern book or any other DRG publications, visit DRGwholesale.com

Every effort has been made to ensure that the instructions in this pattern book are complete and accurate. We cannot, however, take responsibility for human error, typographical mistakes or variations in individual work. Please visit ClotildeCustomerCare.com to check for pattern updates.

ISBN: 978-1-59217-324-2

1 2 3 4 5 6 7 8 9

6

10

13

16

18

20

22

25

28

31

34

37

40

42

44